TEN H○USES

TEN HOUSES

Edited by Oscar Riera Ojeda

Miller / Hull Partnership

First published in the United States of America by:

Rockport Publishers, Inc.

33 Commercial Street

Gloucester, Massachusetts 01930

Telephone: 978-282-9590

Fax: 978-283-2742

Distributed to the book trade and art trade in the United States of America by

North Light Books, an imprint of F & W Publications

1504 Dana Avenue

Cincinnati, Ohio 45207

Telephone: 513-531-2222

Other distribution by

Rockport Publishers Inc.

ISBN 1-56496-450-7

10 9 8 7 6 5 4 3 2 1

Printed in Hong Kong

Cover Photograph: Michaels/Sisson Residence. Photograph by Fred Housel

Back Cover Photographs are of projects on pages (from left, top to bottom) 16, 26, 36, 46, 52, 64, 72, 80, 92, 98

Page 2: Island Cabin. Photograph by Chris Eden. Page 107 Partners Photograph by Ann Kim

Contents

Foreword

by Rodolphe el-Khoury

The abstract propositions of modern architecture touted a revolutionary reorganization of the practice of life. But these visions remained aloof. The idea of realism was rehabilitated in the late 1950s in an attempt to ground architectural dreams in existing norms—and to fashion them from what was culturally believable.

We are at a similar turning point. A new and strategically "realist" architecture—the staple of The Miller/Hull Partnership—is poised to challenge the more esoteric architectural idioms of our own day. The buildings of this new realism are grounded in the language of the familiar. Instead of being roughly translated from the latest scientific, artistic, or philosophical propositions, they find a solid source for invention in known and accessible building types and conventions.

The houses designed by Miller/Hull are simple enclosures, skillfully scaled and crafted for domestic programs. They represent a kind of functional sustainability. Versatile rather than dogmatic, they welcome different modes of occupancy and allow for a variety of interior decorative treatments. But this is not to suggest that these modest houses lack style, that they do not project a particular taste or an articulate aesthetic sensibility. Rather, this is to point out that Miller/Hull's houses—take the Sugden Residence as an example—have the virtue of restraint. Unlike more fashionable and consistently strident idioms, these buildings switch from attitudes of effacement to those of gestural hyperbole in designated emblematic moments. The Sugden house is unlikely to be compromised or corrupted by its occupants' customizing touches since its conventionally designed rooms do not aspire to a dogmatic stylistic integrity or tell any one particular story.

"We will not allow ourselves to be tyrannized by our own rooms any longer." Spoken almost a century ago against the intransigence of Jugenstil, Adolf Loos' protest has yet to lose its currency. The same sentiment is at the core of Miller/Hull's practice: its houses have much to offer in superlative beauty, solidity, and commodity. The firm's gifts are best appreciated when its deliberately muted plans let us "rule again within our four walls."

Island Cabin, Decatur Island, Washington

Rodolphe el-Khoury is an architect, critic, and historian who teaches at the Harvard Graduate School of Design

Campbell Residence, Yakima Valley, Washington

Camarda Residence, Vashon Island, Washington

Marquand Retreat, Naches Valley, Washington

Introduction

by Aaron Betsky

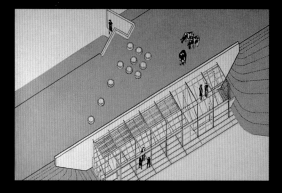

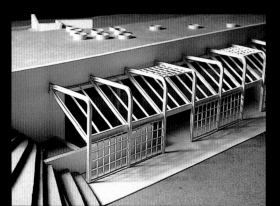

Home is no longer where the heart is. The family homestead is not the center of a universe of change anymore. Few Americans grow up and grow old in the houses in which they were born. A house is, instead, a temporary haven from an outside world that most of us experience as hostile. It is a bunker, fed by electricity, telephone lines, security systems, sewer lines, and above all else, the flood of data that comes in through televisions and computers. The American home has become a retreat into blank and bland isolation.

This is not good news for architects. For them, the American home has been a site of experimentation ever since (and even before) Jefferson turned Monticello into an experimental laboratory in the effort to build a nation. The single-family home was a place in which designers could test ideas about habitation, technology, and our relationship to the land and to the network of social relations.

The sheltering roof, the wings extending into space, the assemblage of parts, the gathering around a core of services, and all the other themes that move through the work of architects such as Frank Lloyd Wright have helped define American culture as much as the syncopation of jazz or the thrust of skyscrapers.

Now architects must operate in a more limited territory. They can engage in experimentation only if the home is either a second home or a site of hybrid needs. In the first case, the house becomes a site of fantasy. It becomes a construction that acts as a projection of how the client sees his or her relation to all the issues of habitation, landscape, and social definition that we usually see as being articulated by the home. Once the house is no longer charged with being the still center of existence, but is instead a place of escape, the possible can once again be constructed. Alternatively, if the house has to combine work and living or somehow engages the land directly through farming, the house can take on the character of a compound whose parts have an active relationship to each other and to their site.

Left: Hansen Residence, Moses Lake, Washington; an earth-sheltered, passive solar house.
Opposite page, left: Kemmick Residence, Cle Elum, Washington; a passive solar mountain house.
Opposite page, center and right: Mercy Residence, Lake Marcel, Washington; an earth-sheltered residence in deep forest.

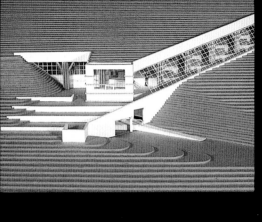

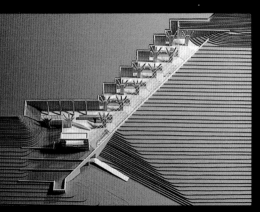

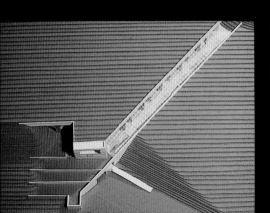

The Seattle architecture firm The Miller/Hull Partnership is lucky enough to find itself designing houses in these two categories. Many of their homes lie scattered around the islands that make up Puget Sound, and are second homes. The ones that are primary residences, such as the Camarda Residence (1994), which also has a vineyard on the property, and the Bainbridge House and Studio (1993), which includes a studio compound, fall into the second category of combinations of home and workplace noted above. As a result, Miller/Hull has been free to engage in experimentation. The architects have taken this opportunity to heart, and have developed their responses from the most basic of ingredients to highlight an openness toward the landscape that their work inspires. Miller/Hull designs houses that are made out of the material that dominates their landscape—wood—but that do not try to evoke the trees themselves. Instead, their houses act as sympathetic frameworks in which the owners can inhabit and see the great Northwest woods (and sometimes the grassy plains of eastern Washington state) through the framework of the rational reduction of residential inhabitation that culture engenders and architects build for us.

Thus there is little spatial complexity in these houses. They are essentially cabins. When they become larger, they are aggregates of simple spaces, with little emphasis on transitions or sequences. They are modernist lofts that the architects have transported to the woods. Miller/Hull has lined all the services up along one line or corner, and then strung the rooms out in simple lines. They keep walls to a minimum. This leaves the structure as the most important part of the building, but Miller/Hull does not go in for an expressionist attitude toward these elements. Instead, they continue the American tradition of using wood construction as the basis for spatial orientation and ornament. They allow the meeting of structural elements to become the focal points of the spaces and play the flat planes of cladding against the particularity of framing

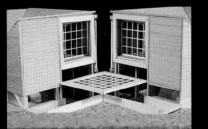

Left: Bloome Residence, Seattle, Washington; the competition winner for a residence on a steep hillside
Opposite page, center and bottom: Sugden Residence, Redmond, Washington; a three-story, wood-frame pavilion set against concrete block service core.
Opposite page, top: Roundy Residence, Ebey's Landing national historic district, Widby Island, Washington.

members. Each piece remains as an exposition of its own nature and its role in the making of the house. Miller/Hull's own contribution to this modern Stick style vernacular is the use of bright colors, such off-the-shelf components as garage doors, and an almost Japanese sensibility about joinery.

They developed this way of making houses from the simple models and recipe books developed by the likes of Charles Moore in the 1960s. They then honed that master's hedonistic, ad hoc, playful attitude towards placemaking on the ecological grindstone of 1970s environmentalism. Miller/Hull's early houses were sheltered in the earth. They were solar collectors, and otherwise justified their occupation of the land through a wise husbanding of resources. Structure was simple, the buildings followed the land, and technology stood exposed as a clarification of what humans do to occupy the land.

Year in and year out, the architects of Miller/Hull keep going back to the small island of Decatur to hone these traditions into simple cabins that exist in a place where there are no cars and no cities. Examples include Gorton/Bounds Cabin (1989), the Novotny Cabin (1990), and the anonymous cabin of 1994. In this fantastic realm, their wood grids, shed roofs, and expressed structure create not only frames but also something approaching a child's drawing of a house. Miller/Hull has caught the essence of the "cabin in the woods" to which one escapes to find one's self framed by all the necessities of life and the clarifying order of an architecture, yet free from imposed plans and the complexities of layered compositions or laws.

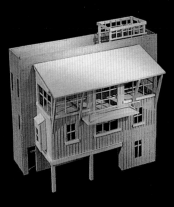

The work is resolutely not grand or imposing. Their houses are often small commissions, and even when they are larger, the architects break them up into pieces. This is not work that you enter or experience in a consciously deliberate manner. Instead, you often slip in along the long axis, or into a facade in which the front door is noted, but not exaggerated. There is usually one large room (sometimes the only space), but it is open to the surrounding rooms. There are few twists of geometry. Simplicity and clarity reign. Only the grand sweep of the Poschman House (1991), with its spaces stepping down the slope and its steel beams marching around the curve, has any aspirations to a sense of grandeur.

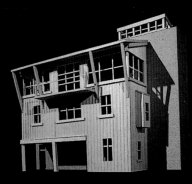

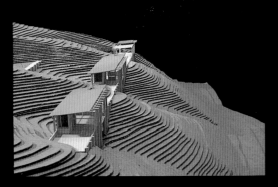

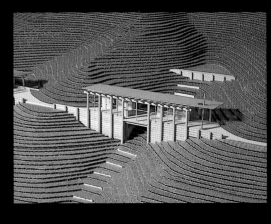

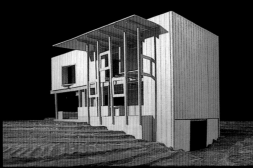

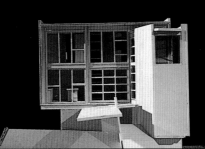

The Ching Cabin, a long "dogtrot" house imported from the Southeast to Puget Sound, is more typical. The recently completed building is tiny, basically one room. The kitchen and bathroom string their appliances along one wall. A garden shed takes up almost a third of the length of the house. The whole house is just a shed, except that the grids of wood and the arrangement of the windows give it an articulation that speaks of human habitation.

The Camarda House blows this same simple scheme up to a larger scale. One does enter through a somewhat formal front door, rather than slipping in along the long axis, but one immediately confronts storage closets that make one move to the left or right before entering the main space. The rooms follow each other to either side of this loft with simple precision. The house evokes an Italian palazzo only in the slight curve of its roof and its coloring. The Bainbridge House and Studio, whose studio stands off at an angle to the main house, shows their work at its hybrid best.

Perhaps the most refined design, though, is the tiny Marquand Retreat of 1992. It sits in a landscape devoid of trees, and is a block bunker that closes down with steel shutters when it is not in use. When open, it is no more than a place of shade pinned down to the land by a tower housing a bathroom surmounted by a water storage tank. Technology, frame, and place all have an elemental presence. It is almost as if the isolation of this particular piece—in an area that is far removed from the landscape in which Miller/Hull usually works—clarifies the basic element of the architect's recipe into its clearest form.

There is a sense of repetition about the work of Miller/Hull, both inside each house and from design to design. Though the partners are quick to point out the differences in the work they each do, one recognizes a Miller/Hull house

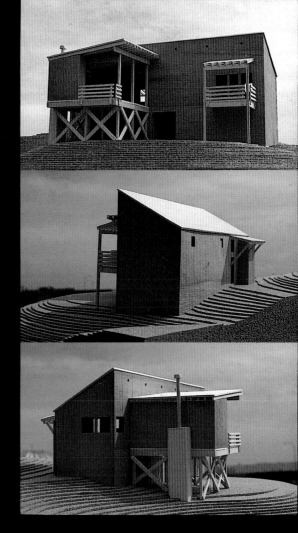

Opposite page, top: *Grande Ronde Ranch, Asotin County, Washington; three pavilions connect the land without altering the watershed.*
Opposite page, center: *Roddy/Bale Residence, Phantom Lake, Washington; a waterfront home with open plan and exterior entry space.*
Opposite page, bottom: *Michaels/Sisson Residence, Mercer Island, Washington; a minimal urban dwelling raised into the trees.*
Right: *Marks Residence, Vashon Island, Washington; simple sheds capture outdoor living areas.*

immediately. This is not a bad thing. The architects have developed a methodology that allows them to respond to client and setting. They do this without having each design succumb to a specificity that would drown out a sense of the shared stylistic and—through that cultural or, if one wants to be relativizing—lifestyle sensibility that the architecture can and does establish.

Yet there is a virtue to their concentration on houses. In these second homes and hybrid compounds, Miller/Hull establishes prototypes for deracinated lives. Instead of pretending that we belong to the land or the community, these houses actively create a scenario in which we can begin to establish such relationships. It is a wonderful dream of returning—however cynically, and however plugged into the networks of dissipated economic structures—to a moment of clarity in a particular place. They make homesteads for modern pioneers in the sprawl that is invading even the sylvan settings of the Pacific Northwest.

The advantage of the situation in which Miller/Hull find themselves is that they are able to address this larger situation and within it make simple things well. Without falling into fetishization or needless complexity, they compose the most basic elements we need to live and then give them a frame that allows us to understand the place of such activities in their human and physical context. They make fantastic houses that are not castles, but all American homes. It is a pleasant dream of inhabitation, an architectural reverie that affirms the possibility and the pleasure of dreaming in sticks and stones.

Left and Right: Poschman Residence, Orcas Island, Washington; glazed public spaces framed by steel bents nest against the long, wood-framed service bar.

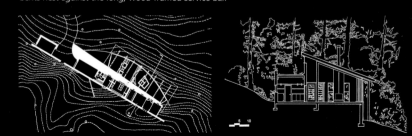

Aaron Betsky is curator of architecture and design at San Francisco's Museum of Modern Art and is a regular contributor to numerous international design and architecture magazines. He has written two books: Queer Space (William Morrow & Company 1997) and Violated Perfection (Rizzoli 1991).

Novotny Cabin

Decatur Island, Washington

Located on Decatur Island in the San Juan Island chain, this cabin perches on a steeply sloping site that abruptly terminates at a rock cliff on the water's edge. The 840-square-foot (78-square-meter) structure is entered from a bridge onto the upper floor living/kitchen/dining area.

Glass surrounds all four sides and deep, six-foot (two-meter) overhangs extend out to protect the outdoor decks. The lower floor elevations are solid with "punched" windows at the built-in beds. The upper floor post-and-beam construction extends out of the solid lower walls. The building's thirteen-foot (four-meter) width provides exterior elevations reminiscent of forest service lookout stations. The wood brackets hold up the roof cantilever, and act as stiffeners against seismic forces and wind.

Above: *The angled members of the heavy, timber-braced frame provide shear and support the broad overhangs that cover the deck and shade the glazing.*

Opposite Page: *Continuous glazing wraps the upper floor of the cabin, and floats the roof above the solid base.*

5   10

East Elevation

Section Facing South

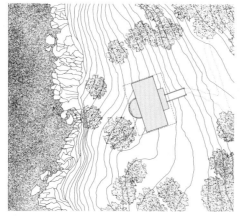

Site Plan

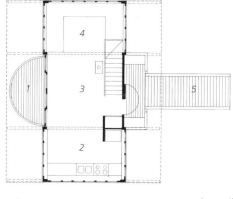

Upper Floor Plan

1. Deck

2. Kitchen

3. Dining Room

4. Living Room

5. Bridge

6. Bedroom

7. Bed

8. Flexible Space

9. Bathroom

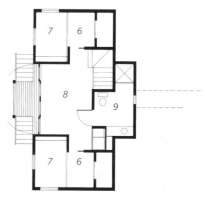

Lower Floor Plan

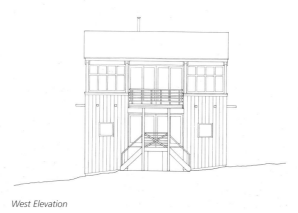

West Elevation

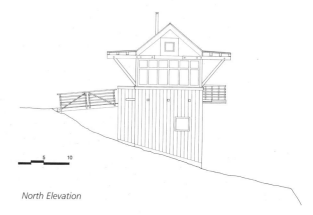

North Elevation

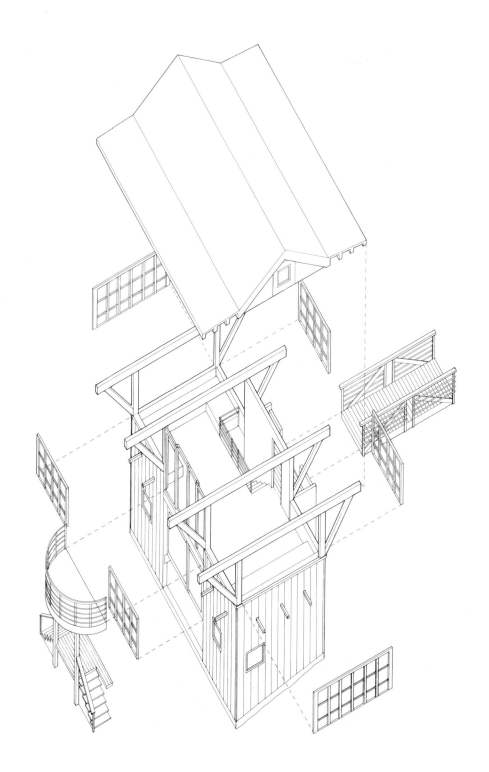

Right: *The transparency of the upper floor is maintained through the kitchen by attaching the open shelving directly to the mullions.*

Opposite Page: *Exposed, simply detailed connections provide both visual interest and structural clarity to the cabin's interior.*

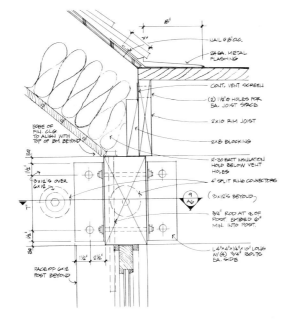

NAIL @ 8' O.C.

24 GA. METAL FLASHING

CONT. VENT SCREEN

(2) 1½"⌀ HOLES FOR EA. JOIST SPACE

2x10 RIM JOIST

2x8 BLOCKING

R-30 BATT INSULATION HOLD BELOW VENT HOLES

4" SPLIT RING CONNECTORS

(3x12's BEYOND)

¾" ROD AT ₵ OF POST EMBED 6" MIN. INTO POST.

L 4"x 4"x ¼"x 10" LONG W/ (4) ¾" BOLTS EA. SIDE

EDGE OF FIN. CLG. FIN. CLG. TO ALIGN WITH TOP OF BM. BEYOND

3x12's OVER 6x12

9
A6

FACE OF 6x12 POST BEYOND

8"   4"

8   TYP. HEAD

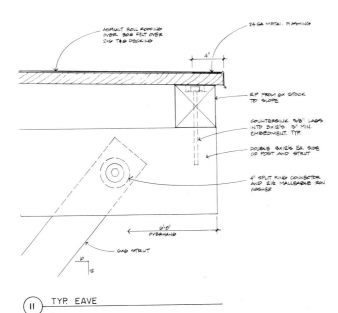

ASPHALT ROLL ROOFING OVER 30# FELT OVER 2x6 T&G DECKING

24 GA. METAL FLASHING

RIP FROM 6x STOCK TO SLOPE

COUNTERSINK ⅝" LAGS INTO 3x12's 5" MIN. EMBEDMENT. TYP.

DOUBLE 3x12's EA. SIDE OF POST AND STRUT

4" SPLIT RING CONNECTOR AND 2½" MALLEABLE IRON WASHER

4"

6'-0" OVERHANG

12

6x6 STRUT

11   TYP. EAVE

Gorton/Bounds Cabin

Decatur Island, Washington

Asteep forest clearing located on a small island in the San Juan Island Chain set the design direction for this small cabin for a family of three. The site, a 100-foot- (30-meter) diameter circle, is part of a planned island development where special care has been taken to isolate each circular site and to take advantage of other terrain. Views open not only to the forest but to a spectacular panorama of the islands as far away as Canada. Access to the cabin is by a trail; all construction materials had to be barged to the site.

Compactness, economy, and a desire to feel open to the site were paramount considerations expressed by the family. The 600-square-foot (56-square-meter) structure contrasts between a core and an open roof structure. The core, 90 inches (229 cm) wide, acts as a stiffened structural box. This compact limitation results in small, cozy areas for one sleeping room, two sleeping lofts reached by ladder, a bath, entry, storage, and a kitchen.

In contrast to the enclosed core, the living and dining space—under a roof canopy of heavy timber beams—feels expansive, opening out toward the views. The core, with its framed openings and entry niche, acts as a backdrop to the living space. An infill system of wood-framed, double-glazed, roll-up garage door sections completes the enclosure. This very inexpensive system utilizes full-height operable panels for natural ventilation. All joints are caulked and covered with wood batts to reduce heat loss.

Section Facing North

South Elevation

West Elevation

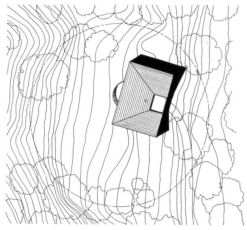

Site Plan

1. Porch
2. Dining Room
3. Living Room
4. Kitchen
5. Storage
6. Bathroom
7. Bedroom
8. Ladder to Loft Above

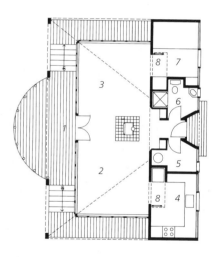

Floor Plan

East Elevation

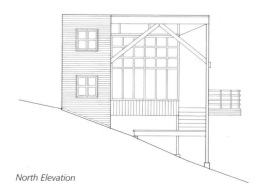

North Elevation

Left: *The cantilevered deck connects the two main structural frames while extending the living space out into the landscape toward panoramic views of the San Juan Islands.*

Opposite Page: *Projecting roof framing lifts up toward the view and provides shading for the generous glazing.*

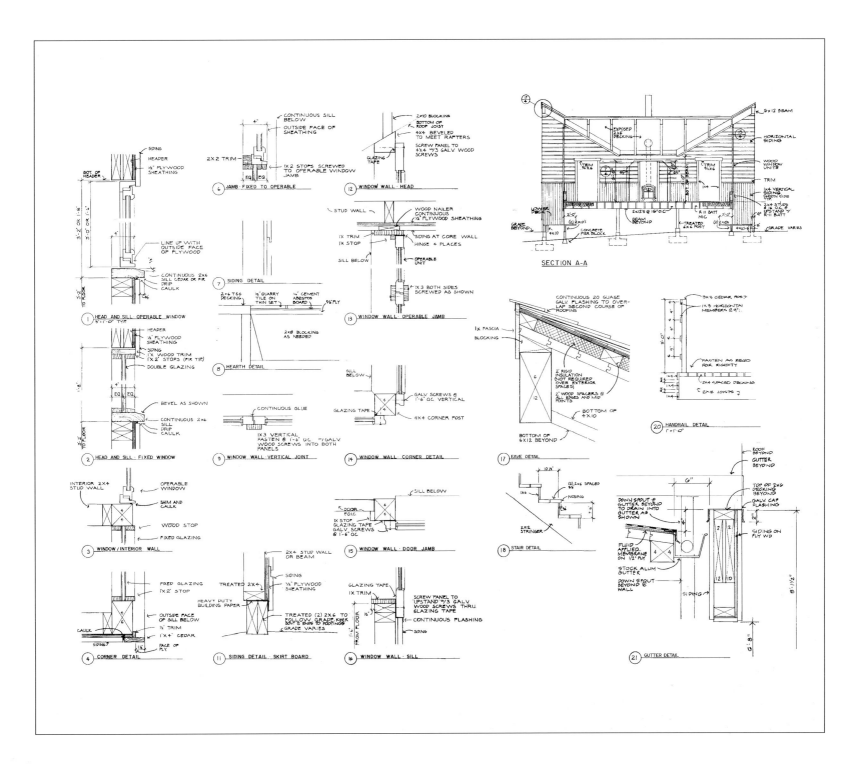

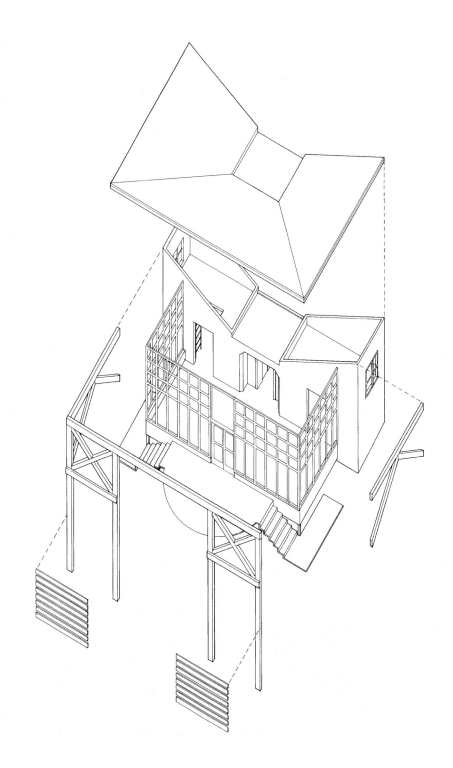

Marquand Retreat

Naches River Valley, Washington

The Naches River west of Yakima flows from the Cascade Mountains to the east and has carved out a beautiful valley rimmed by basalt cliffs. Attracted to the arid climate, the client, a busy Seattle publisher, purchased a 200-acre (81-hectare) "bowl" on the slope of a mountain. The site faces down into the river valley and cliffs beyond, and is used for weekend getaways. The owner set the design challenge: to construct a limited, two-room program using materials that were resistant to fire, wind, and intruders. The design had to respond to the potential for both blistering heat and freezing cold. However, the owner still wanted natural light and an architecture that expressed the raw quality of the site.

The structure was conceived as a thin metal roof floated across a basic concrete block rectangle. The floating roof provides a shaded porch to the south, clerestory window slots at the main shell, and a covered path out to the water cistern tower to the rear of the building. A ten-foot- (three-meter-) square opening faces south under the porch with two full-size sliding doors hung on a track running the entire length of the wall. With one door screened and one glazed, the owner can customize the proportion of open ventilation to glazed area. The material palette consists of concrete block, and structural wood decking with metal roofing and wood windows. Since the 450-square-foot (42-square-meter) structure lacks permanent power, a wood stove effectively provides heat. The cistern is currently filled by a water truck, with plans for a well to be dug in the future .

Above: Small "punched" openings in the east and west walls capture select views of the site while being easily protected when the cabin is unoccupied.

Opposite Page: The sturdy structure sits stoically within the basalt-rimmed desert valley in eastern Washington State.

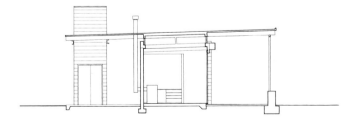

Section Facing East

5 10

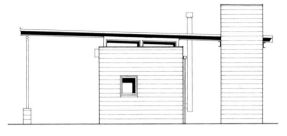

East Elevation

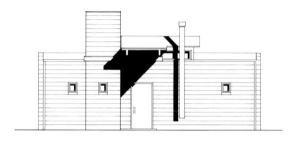

North Elevation

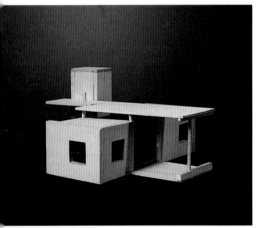

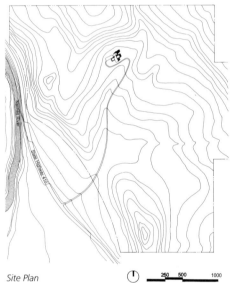

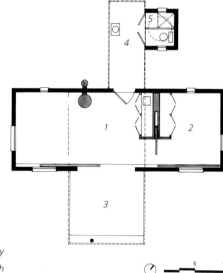

Site Plan

250   500   1000

Plan

1. Main Room
2. Bed Room
3. Porch
4. Covered Walkway
5. Water Tower/Bath

5   10

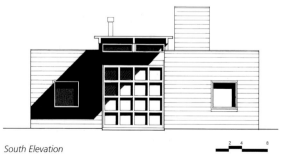

South Elevation

2 4   8

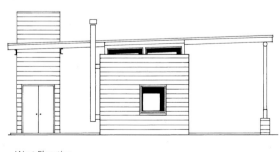

West Elevation

This Page: *All the openings are operable for natural light and ventilation in this variable and harsh climate, and all can be closed off against weather and intruders when the building is empty.*

Opposite Page: *The project is an exercise in elemental forms that suit their purpose— a tower bath and cistern, a box for living, and a simple plane roof with one column for shelter.*

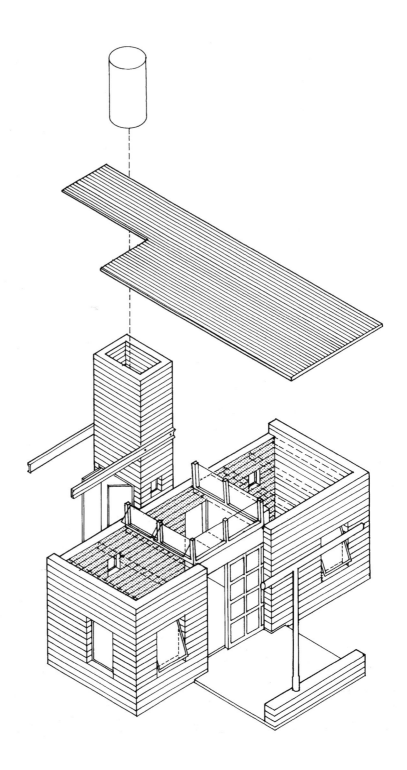

This Page: *Twin doors of glass and screen on a single track allow the occupant to modulate the proportion of ventilation to suit conditions.*

Opposite Page: *Kept small, the punched windows maximize the mass of the concrete masonry walls. The sliding doors slip over and are seen through the small front windows from the exterior.*

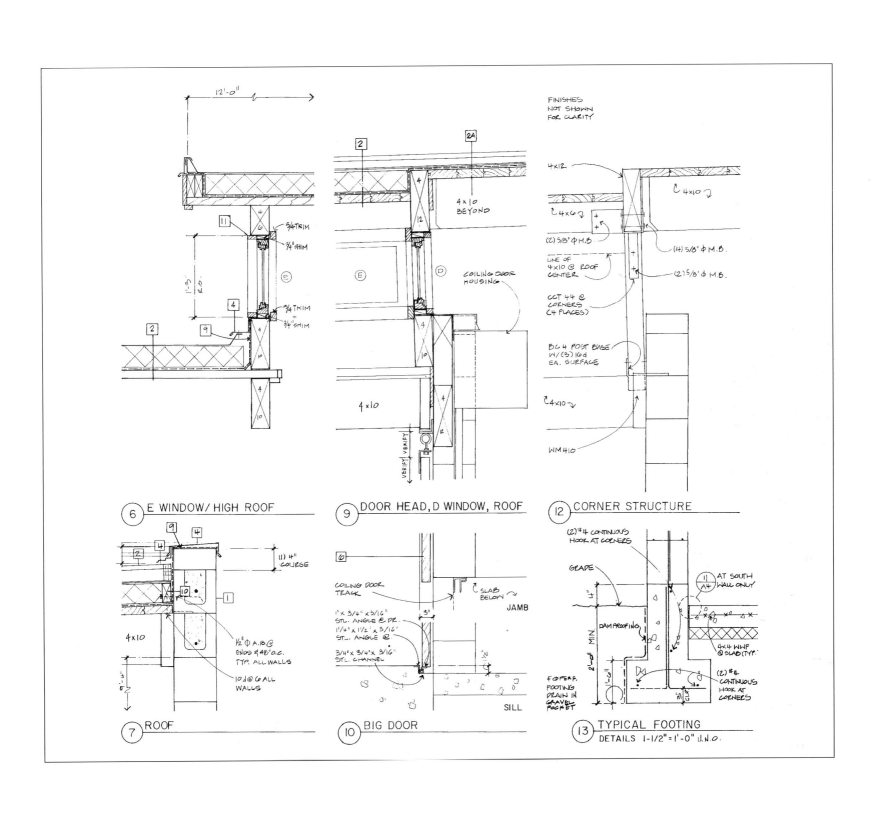

12'-0"

FINISHES
NOT SHOWN
FOR CLARITY

2   2A

4x10
BEYOND

3/4 TRIM
3/4 SHIM

3/4 TRIM
3/4 SHIM

COILING DOOR
HOUSING

E   E   D

4x10

4x10

4x12

⌐4x10⌐

⌐4x6⌐

(2) 5/8"⌀ M.B.

(4) 5/8"⌀ M.B.

LINE OF
4x10 @ ROOF
CENTER

(2) 5/8"⌀ M.B.

CCT 44 @
CORNERS
(4 PLACES)

BC 4 POST BASE
W/ (3) 16d
EA. SURFACE

⌐4x10⌐

WM410

VERIFY   VERIFY

⑥ E WINDOW/ HIGH ROOF   ⑨ DOOR HEAD, D WINDOW, ROOF   ⑫ CORNER STRUCTURE

(1) 4"
COURSE

4x10

1/2"⌀ A.B. @
ENDS & 48"o.c.
TYP. ALL WALLS

10d @ 6 ALL
WALLS

⑦ ROOF

6

COILING DOOR
TRACK

SLAB
BELOW

JAMB

1" x 3/4" x 3/16"
STL. ANGLE @ DR.
1 1/4" x 1 1/2" x 3/16"
STL. ANGLE @
3/4" x 3/4" x 3/16"
STL. CHANNEL

3"

1/2"

SILL

⑩ BIG DOOR

(2) #4 CONTINUOUS
HOOK AT CORNERS

GRADE

DAMPROOFING

4"

2'-0" MIN

1'-0"

FO PERF.
FOOTING
DRAIN IN
GRAVEL
POCKET

3" CLR

1/A4 AT SOUTH
WALL ONLY

4x4 WWF
@ SLAB (TYP.)

(2) #4
CONTINUOUS
HOOK AT
CORNERS

⑬ TYPICAL FOOTING
DETAILS 1-1/2"=1'-0" U.N.O.

Grand Coulee Residence

Electric City, Washington

This full-time residence is designed for a 2-acre (0.8-hectare) site near Grand Coulee Dam in Eastern Washington. The small (1,200-square-foot/111-square-meter) structure sits on a gentle rise in the desert landscape dominated by an 800-foot (244-meter) rock coulee wall some 500 yards (457 meters) east of the site.

The house was conceived as both a refuge from the harsh desert environment and an open camp. A board-formed concrete bunker provides space for cooking, sleeping, bathing and a private study. Two glass-enclosed rooms project out from the concrete shell: a sitting space to the west with a view of nearby Banks Lake, and a dining space to the east. The roof on the dining structure projects up to gesture to the mass of the rock wall. The owner's car is to be parked at the south end of the structure, under the projecting roof that slides out between the flanking walls of the box.

The interiors are minimal: all furniture is built-in with the exception of a long free-standing table and its chairs in the dining space. Ashlar-patterned stone floors are used in the open sitting and dining spaces, and hardwood floor in the concrete shell portion. The concrete walls are exposed on the interior to reflect the rocky nature of the natural landscape.

This Page: The house is an elongated simple bunker sitting on a high desert plateau with limited fenestration.

Opposite Page: East and west elevations are dominated by board-formed concrete walls that protect the building from the harsh desert climate.

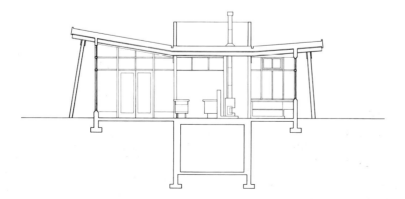

Section Facing South

5   10

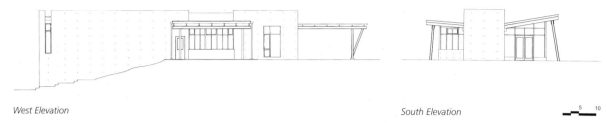

West Elevation

South Elevation

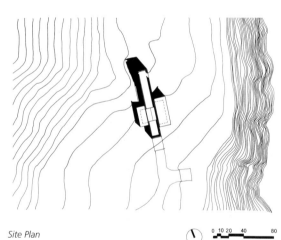

Site Plan

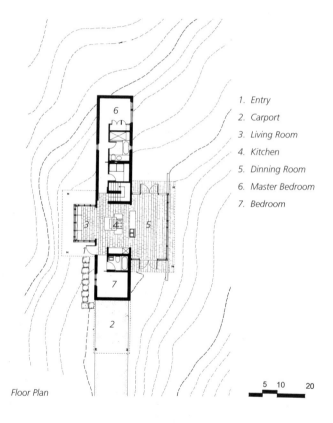

1. Entry
2. Carport
3. Living Room
4. Kitchen
5. Dinning Room
6. Master Bedroom
7. Bedroom

Floor Plan

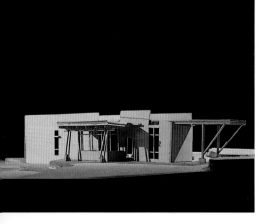

North Elevation

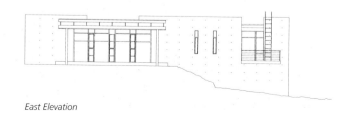

East Elevation

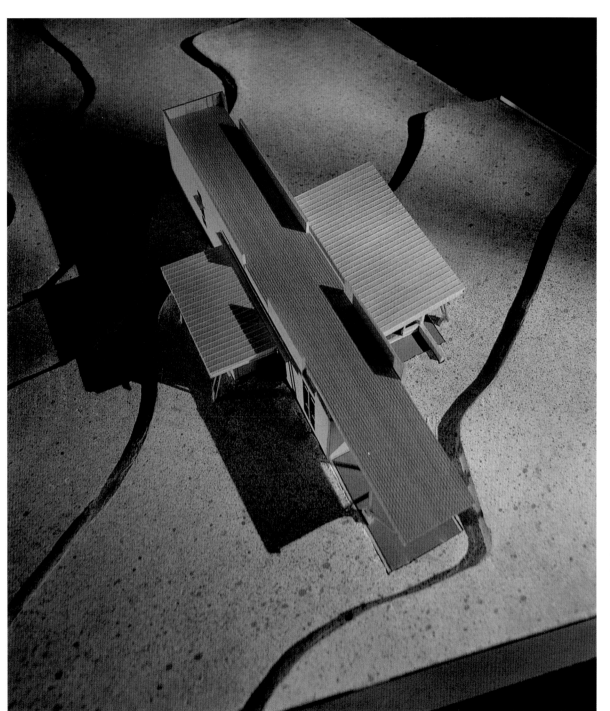

This Page: *The long, flat concrete form of the building holds the service spaces and parallels the cliff wall to the east. Glass pavilions containing the public spaces seem to slide out of the concrete mass.*

Opposite Page: *Simple forms contrast with the harsh, highly textured landscape.*

Right: *The simple block form of the house holds its own against the massive verticality of the Coulee wall.*

Opposite Page: *Component parts meet around the central space of the residence, juxtaposing contrasting materials, two structural systems, and various spatial types.*

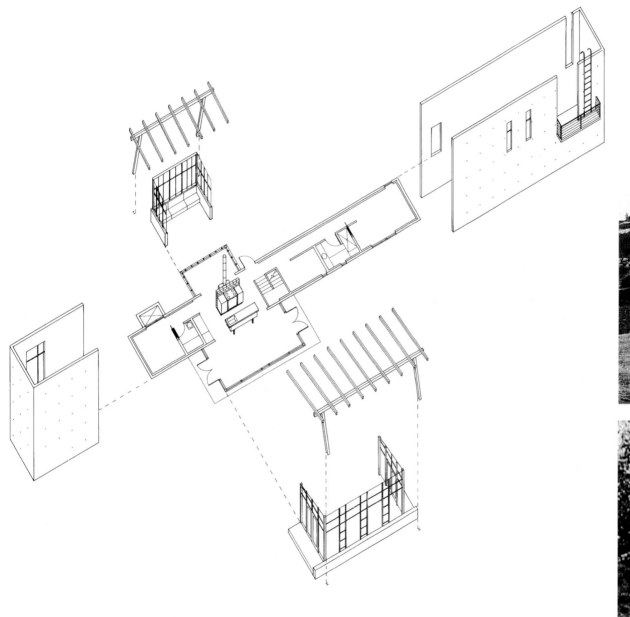

Bainbridge House and Studio

Bainbridge Island, Washington

Situated on 2.5 acres (1 hectare), this 2,600-square-foot (242-square-meter) house with a detached 1,000-square-foot (93-square-meter) studio sits on a gentle slope facing a meadow surrounded by lush woods. Contrasting with the natural environment, this pair of complementary structures creates a modern expression using industrial materials of steel and stucco.

A linear "spine-wall," surfaced in charcoal gray stucco inside and out, runs the length of the main house and projects out at the south end to support the steel entry canopy. Major functions are housed in distinct volumes, including the living dining space with a eighteen-foot- (five-meter-) high ceiling, and are connected by an interior circulation system along the wall. A large kitchen faces the south entry and creates a strong object within the landscape through the use of a large skylight monitor projecting above its cubic volume.

The open-plan detached studio features conference space, work area, reception and storage areas linearly arranged. The careful placement of the studio in relation to the house allows views into the forest from both buildings, while delineating an enclosed, private meadow room.

Above: *The main residence sits in contrast to the landscape as an aggregation of utilitarian boxes arranged along a linear spine-wall.*

Opposite Page: *The graphic quality of the kitchen "box" with its projecting skylight formalizes the entry facade.*

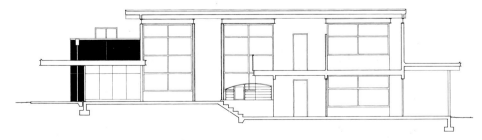

Section Facing East

5   10

Second Floor Plan

1. Master Bedroom
2. Bedroom
3. Bath

First Floor Plan

1. Entry
2. Kitchen
3. Living / Dining
4. Guest Room
5. Bath
6. Utility Room
7. Study

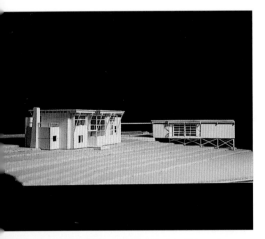

Studio

1. Reception
2. Work Area
3. Conference
4. Bath
5. Storage

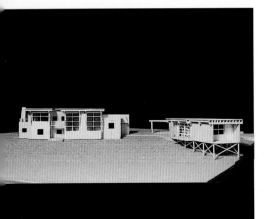

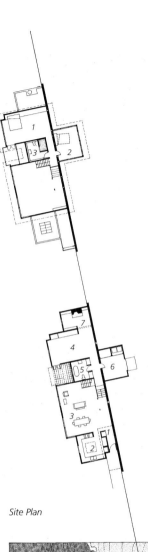

10 20 40

Site Plan

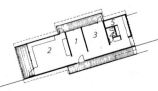

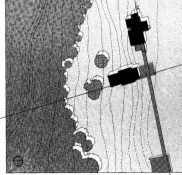

East Elevation

Southwest Corner from Studio

West Elevation from Woods

North Elevation

North Elevation of Studio

Northwest Corner of Studio

South Elevation of Studio

Southeast Corner of Studio

East Elevation of Studio

Right: Major functions are expressed with distinct volumes. For example, the double-height living space is separated from the master bedroom and study element by the recessed deck and patio.

Opposite Page: The main house is grounded to the site with its structural slab on grade foundation, while the studio, elevated on columns, floats over the landscape.

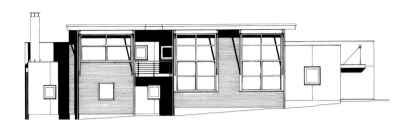

West Elevation

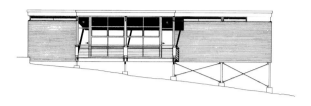

North Elevation

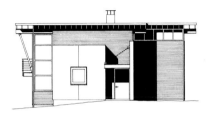

South Elevation

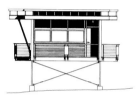

West Elevation

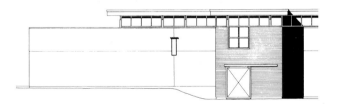

East Elevation

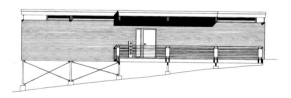

South Elevation

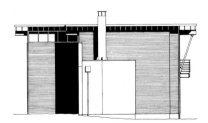

North Elevation

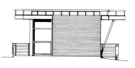

East Elevation

5 10   20

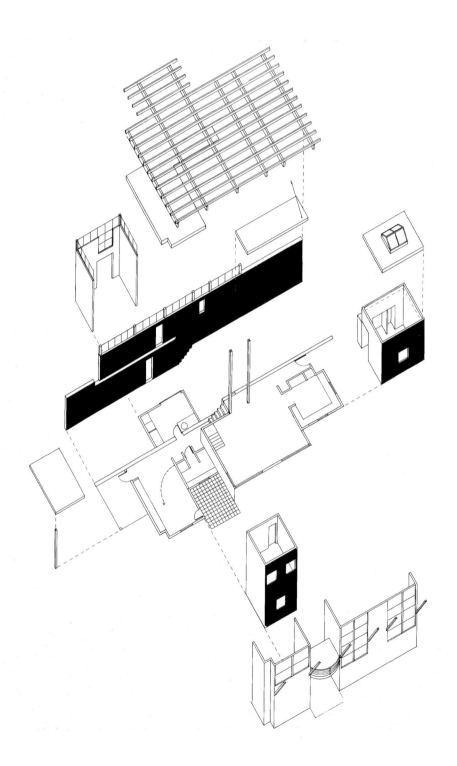

Left: The sweeping arch of the stair railing and its lightly tied planes of plywood float above the simple lines of the stairs, providing a focal point within the simple volume.

Opposite Page: A solid storage unit divides the kitchen and entry spaces while contrasting with the tall, thin columns along the circulation zone. A window dropped below the clerestory allows a framed view into the forest from the second bedroom.

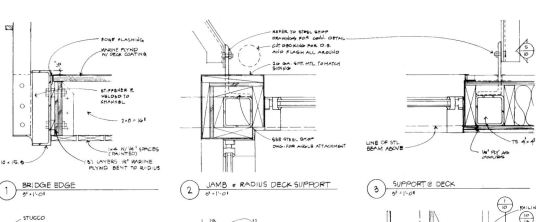

① BRIDGE EDGE
3" = 1'-0"

EDGE FLASHING
MARINE PLYWD W/ DECK COATING
STIFFENER R WELDED TO CHANNEL
2×8 ~ 16"
C10×15.3
1×4 W/ 1/4" SPACES (PAINTED)
(3) LAYERS 1/2" MARINE PLYWD BENT TO RADIUS

② JAMB @ RADIUS DECK SUPPORT
3" = 1'-0"

REFER TO STEEL SHOP DRAWINGS FOR CONN. DETAIL. CUT DECKING FOR D.S. AND FLASH ALL AROUND
26 GA. SHT. MTL. TO MATCH SIDING
SEE STEEL SHOP DWG. FOR ANGLE ATTACHMENT

③ SUPPORT @ DECK
3" = 1'-0"

LINE OF STL. BEAM ABOVE
1/2" PLY AS OCCURS
TS 4×4

④ JAMB @ WALL
3" = 1'-0"

STUCCO
CONT. CLEAT EACH SIDE
FLASHING - 26 GA GALVANIZED, CROWNED
FLASHING AT SIDEWALL BEYOND, LAP OVER CAP FLASHING W/ CONT. BEAD OF SEALANT
SHIM TOP PLATE TO SLOPE
3×6 EA SIDE OF T.S. COL @ PB 5×8 AT NAIL ONLY (2×6 TYPICAL)
LINE OF STL BEAM ABOVE
TS 4'×4"

⑤ ELEVATION - SUPPORT @ DECK
3" = 1'-0"

RAILING PE
RAILING STAN. BOLTED TO STIFFNER

⑧ PARAPET @ LIBRARY/KITCHEN
3" = 1'-0"

TORCH DOWN ROOFING, RUN UP BACK SIDE OF PARAPET WALL
R30 RIGID INSUL (TAPERED)
2×6 T&G DECKING
4×8
2×8

⑨ JAMB @ CORNER
3" = 1'-0"

26 GA. SHT. MTL. TO MATCH FIN. OF METAL SIDING
TS 4"×4"
2×6 TYP. U.N.O.
LINE OF STL. BEAM ABOVE
1/2" PLYWD SHEATHING (TYP.)
5/4 × BLOCKING (VERIFY W/ SIDING THICKNESS)
DOWNSPOUT AT SAME SPACING FROM EDGE AS AT DETAIL 2 ABOVE.

⑩ JAMB @ STUCCO WALL
3" = 1'-0"

2×2
CORNER FLASHING
STUCCO

⑬ EDGE @ STAIR LANDING
3" = 1'-0"

LINE OF CARPET
C10×20.7 BOLT TO (2) 2×10's
CAP PE @ WALL. BOLT TO FRAMING BEYOND
(2) 2×10's
2×10's
GWB

⑭ CORNER @ FAMILY RM. TO BATHROOM
3" = 1'-0"

1/2" PLYWD SHEATHING (TYP.)
STUCCO
SEALANT AND BACKER ROD
NEOPRENE CLOSURE @ METAL SIDING END
METAL SIDING

⑮ JAMB @ M.BEDRM. TO BATHROOM
3" = 1'-0"

SILL BELOW
1/2" PLYWD SHEATHING (TYP.)
SEALANT

Ching Cabin

Maury Island, Washington

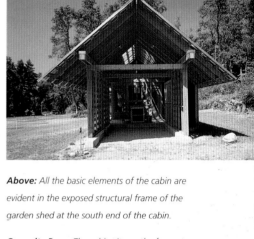

Situated on a small meadow within a ten-acre (four-hectare) site on Vashon Island, a fifteen-minute ferry ride from Seattle, this small (600-square-feet/56-square-meters) cabin and attached garden shed serves as a weekend retreat for a couple and their two children. The cabin was designed to be joined by a larger full-time residence and will provide studio space for the family and guest quarters for visiting friends and relatives. The cabin, the residence, and a third structure—a covered, open-air arbor—will form a string of buildings along the northeast edge of the meadow. All three structures will have access to south and west sunlight and views of the meadow with its two ponds.

The clients have traveled in the far east and were attracted to the simple gable forms and expressed structure of Japanese folk houses. The program was to design a practical, simple, open plan that reflects the casual lifestyle of the family within a clearly articulated volume. The solution essentially creates one room for the communal functions of eating, gathering, and sleeping, with a loft at each end of the main space for the children's sleeping and reading activities. A "garden shed" space concludes the line of the building to the south. Support spaces are lined up in a 42-inch (107-centimeter) service zone at the back of the structure. The main cabin space opens to the meadow through a large double set of tri-fold doors, converting the space to an outdoor room.

The cabin and the garden shed are linked by a continuous corrugated metal roof while separated by an open breezeway for gathering outdoors under cover. Set just apart from the cabin, the well pump house is contained within a corrugated steel culvert and initiates a wall of buildings that will form a constructed edge to the natural meadow.

Above: *All the basic elements of the cabin are evident in the exposed structural frame of the garden shed at the south end of the cabin.*

Opposite Page: *The cabin sits on the far east edge of the meadow to catch both the last rays of the day's sun as well as views across the meadow and ponds to the woods beyond.*

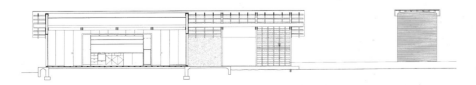

Section Facing East

West Elevation

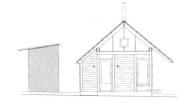

North Elevation

Site Plan

1. Living Room
2. Breezeway
3. Tractor Shed
4. Closet
5. Storage

Floor Plan

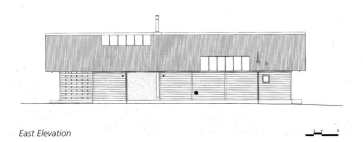

East Elevation

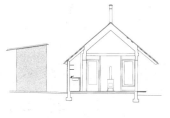

Section Facing South

This Page: *The cabin creates a clear edge for the outdoor gathering space bordered more softly on other sides by the garden, the ponds and the entrance drive.*

Opposite Page: *Translucent panels in plane with the metal roof highlight the exceptions to the linear arrangement of the cabin: the doors onto the deck; the kitchen; and the breezeway. The pump house sits in stark contrast to the cabin in its form, but uses a similar transparent panel for the roof.*

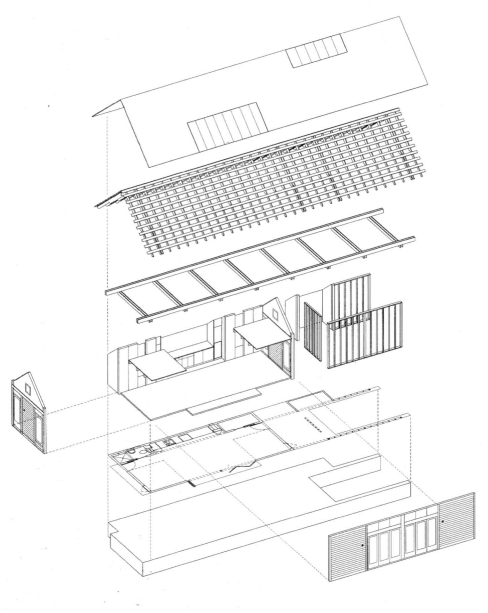

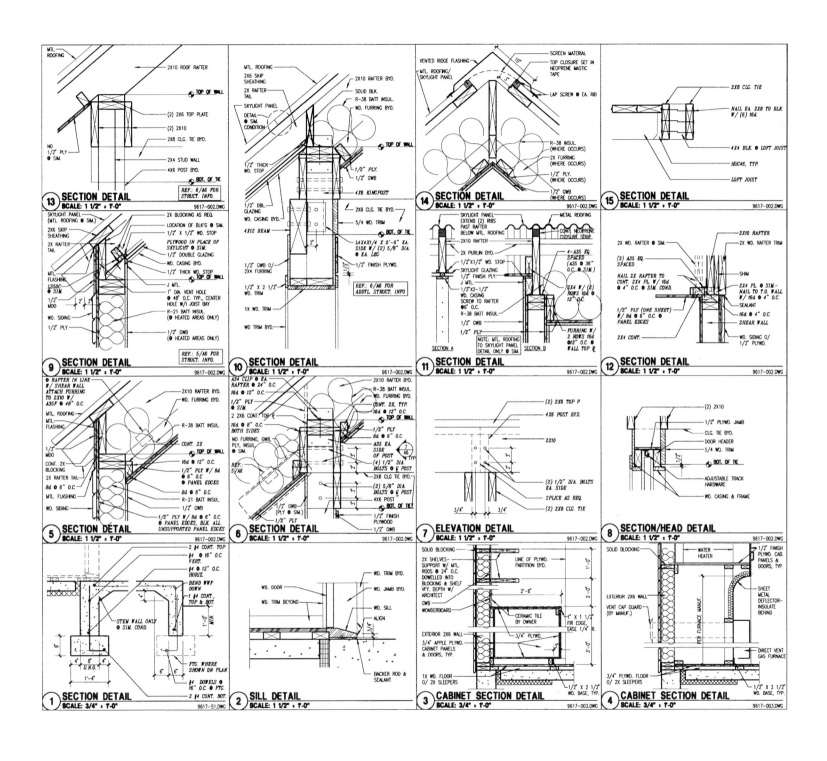

Camarda Residence

Vashon Island, Washington

This home for a family of four is set in five meadow acres (two hectares) in the center of Vashon Island. The owners, an award-winning winemaker and a caterer, are collectors of fine art, have a passion for bold colors, and share an appreciation for the architecture of Aldo Rossi. The client's ideal was a stately Tuscan farmhouse combined with industrial materials and a bold use of color. All these factors were combined into a simple modern design that is also one of the most colorful Miller/Hull has ever designed.

The house and garage back up to the forest wall and are sited parallel to the slope on the low part of the property, facing the meadow and on axis with the winery building placed at the meadow's high point. The 2,200-square-foot (204-square-meter) home consists of a linear form containing bedrooms, bathrooms, and a kitchen intersected by the barrel-vaulted entry and living area. Metal-clad "bookend walls" mark the entries and living room and increase the scale of the building against the tall pines of the forest edge. A verandah runs the length of the bedroom wing, facing the meadow.

Exterior colors include bright yellow stucco, a green metal roof, and steely gray metal fin walls. The interior walls are also brightly painted, and are enhanced by tinted lacquer stains on the doors and all cabinetry. Creative use of common materials and uncommon colors created this modest house with considerable presence for relatively little cost.

Above: One enters the house from a remote parking area through a stand of fir trees. The vertical planes of the entry facade fit the scale of the nearby firs.

Opposite Page: The house is placed at the edge of a large meadow, which now includes the family garden.

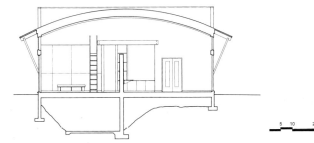

Section Facing North with Wine Cellar Below

5   10   20

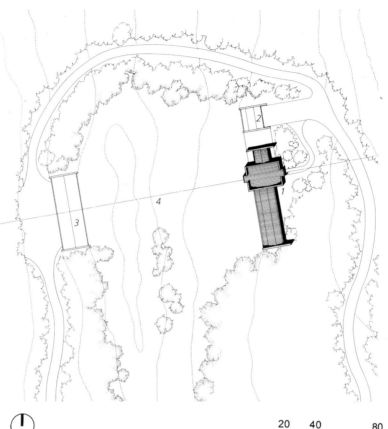

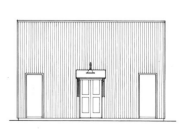

20   40   80

Site Plan

1. House

2. Future Garage

3. Future Winery

4. Meadow/Garden

Floor Plan

1. Main Bedroom   5. Office

2. Bedroom   6. Utility

3. Bedroom   7. Kitchen

4. Living/Dining   8. Future Garage

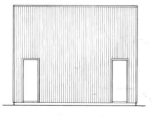

South Elevation

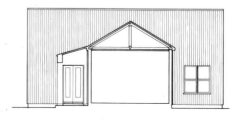

Section Facing North

North Elevation

Left: *The long veranda facing the meadow and winery building beyond opens off the living dining space. The owners' informal style of living works well with the playful use of color.*

Opposite Page: *Small openings emphasize the planar quality of the end walls.*

This Page: The use of color permeates the house on all surfaces. In combination with natural wood and concrete masonry, the material palette is lively and informal.

Opposite Page: The intersection of two forms organizes the house both formally and spatially. The larger volume—containing the living and dining areas—divides the longer volume, separating the kitchen and private functions.

West Elevation

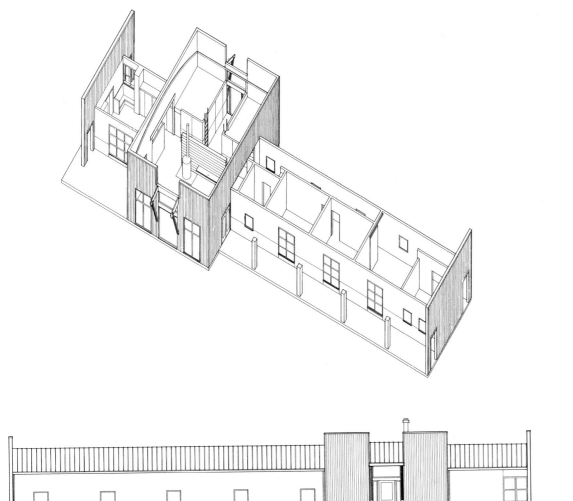

East Elevation

2 4   8

Campbell Residence

Yakima Valley, Washington

The site for this home is an 180-acre (73-hectare) ranch at the base of the Cascade Mountain foothills near the small town of Tieton, Washington. At 1800 feet (549 meters) in elevation, the ranch sits on a plateau, with dramatic views west to the mountains and east to the Naches River Valley. The owners, who currently reside in San Anselmo, California, are third-generation owners of this seventy-five-year-old ranch and orchard; they plan to eventually relocate to the Seattle area. Their desires for the home were twofold: to provide a home base for regular trips to the ranch, and eventually to serve as a second home for extended stays. Prevailing wind was a primary factor in the design of the home, influencing the decision to tuck the house into a hillside for shelter. Further wind protection is gained by the construction of a wall at one end of an open carport, with a large sliding door to access the house or shut out the wind. The wall also provides security, as the owners are absent for much of the time.

The house is split into three primary pieces—the carport and wind protection wall; a small office; and the main house. The outdoor space, framed between the building elements and a large existing ponderosa pine, is the focus of the house. One of the owners, an interior designer, provided immaculately detailed custom cabinetry and fixtures throughout the project.

The building materials are rugged: concrete block walls, used to hold back the hillside, are exposed inside and out. Recycled Douglas fir purlins are set on exposed steel beams and columns that are canted to mimic the old orchard props used to support fruit-laden branches. Indoor and outdoor space are connected by a stained concrete slab which extends out and engages basalt boulders found on the site.

Above: *Building components on the north side turn to face the views of the valley, while the heavy south-facing walls dig into the hill on the windward side.*

Opposite Page: *The view as one makes the passage from the orchard to the sheltered promontory at the entry.*

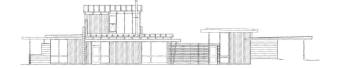

Campbell Residence

1. Carport
2. Office
3. Living/Dining
4. Kitchen
5. Bath
6. Mech./Storage
7. Master Bedroom

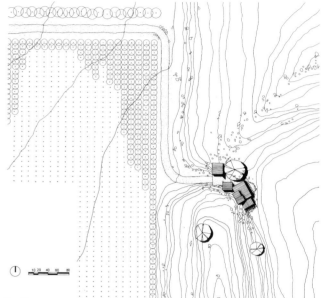

Site Plan

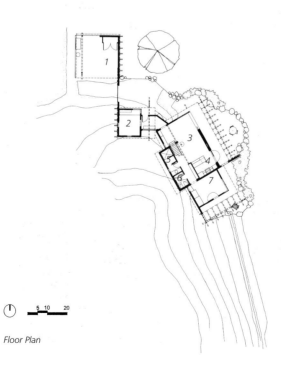

Floor Plan

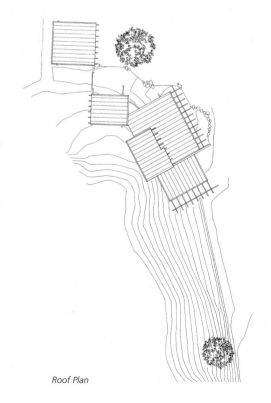

Roof Plan

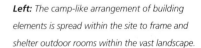

Left: *The camp-like arrangement of building elements is spread within the site to frame and shelter outdoor rooms within the vast landscape.*

Opposite Page: *The house unfolds as it wraps along the hillside, terminating in the outdoor terrace space off the master bedroom.*

Right: *The slab was poured to engage boulders from the site, blurring the edge delineation and contrasting the sleek lines of the steel columns and beams.*

Opposite Page: *Varied elevations share a language of wood boxes, steel framing, concrete block walls, and wood trellis structures.*

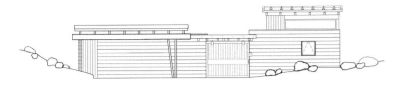

West Elevation

Section Facing South

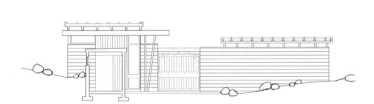

Section Facing West

Section Facing North

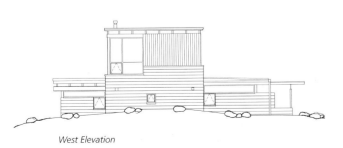

West Elevation

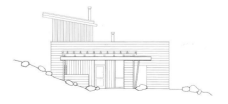

South Elevation

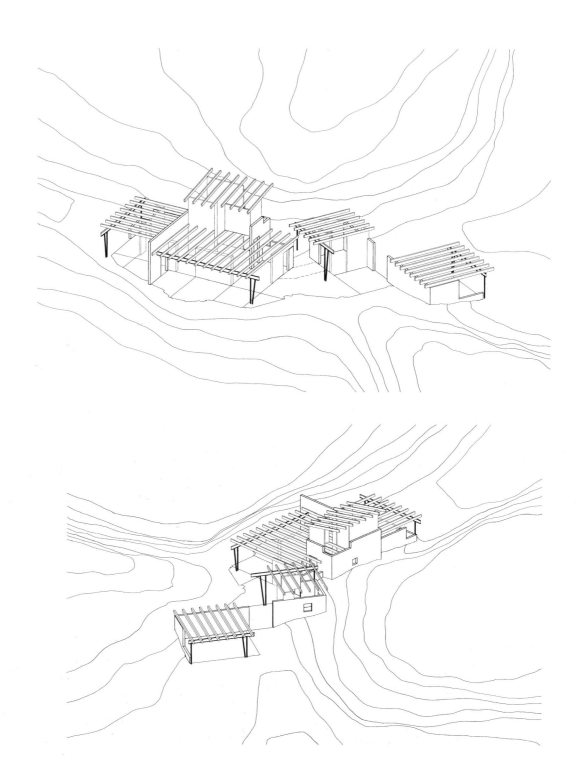

Right: *Each building element was placed in response to the setting, framing a variety of dramatic views.*

Opposite Page: *Careful detailing further emphasizes the tectonic attributes of the building.*

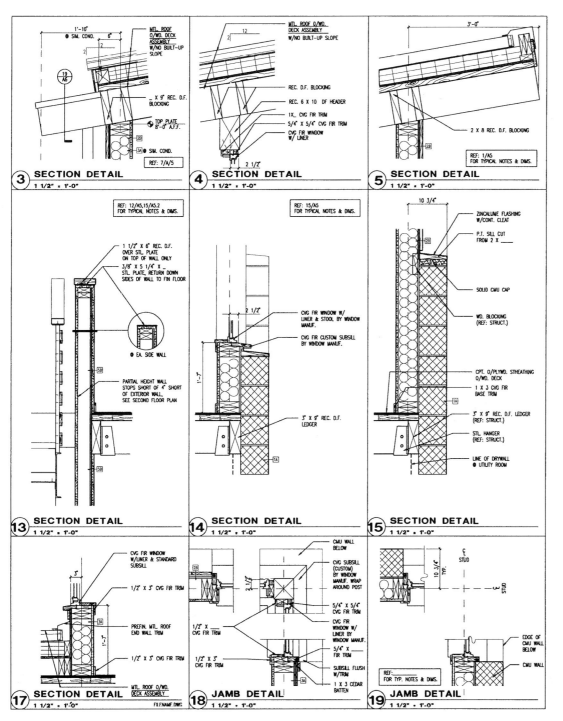

3 SECTION DETAIL
1 1/2" = 1'-0"

MTL. ROOF O/WD. DECK ASSEMBLY W/NO BUILT-UP SLOPE

_ X 9" REC. D.F. BLOCKING

TOP PLATE 8'-0" A.F.F.

SIM. COND.

REF: 7/A/5

4 SECTION DETAIL
1 1/2" = 1'-0"

MTL. ROOF O/WD. DECK ASSEMBLY W/NO BUILT-UP SLOPE

REC. D.F. BLOCKING

REC. 6 X 10 DF HEADER

1X_ CVG FIR TRIM

5/4" X 5/4" CVG FIR TRIM

CVG FIR WINDOW W/ LINER

5 SECTION DETAIL
1 1/2" = 1'-0"

2 X 8 REC. D.F. BLOCKING

REF: 1/A5 FOR TYPICAL NOTES & DIMS.

13 SECTION DETAIL
1 1/2" = 1'-0"

REF: 12/A5,15/A5.2 FOR TYPICAL NOTES & DIMS.

1 1/2" X 6" REC. D.F. OVER STL. PLATE ON TOP OF WALL ONLY

3/8" X 5 1/4" X _ STL. PLATE, RETURN DOWN SIDES OF WALL TO FIN FLOOR

EA. SIDE WALL

PARTIAL HEIGHT WALL STOPS SHORT OF 4" SHORT OF EXTERIOR WALL, SEE SECOND FLOOR PLAN

14 SECTION DETAIL
1 1/2" = 1'-0"

REF: 15/A5 FOR TYPICAL NOTES & DIMS.

CVG FIR WINDOW W/ LINER & STOOL BY WINDOW MANUF.

CVG FIR CUSTOM SUBSILL BY WINDOW MANUF.

3" X 9" REC. D.F. LEDGER

15 SECTION DETAIL
1 1/2" = 1'-0"

ZINCALUME FLASHING W/CONT. CLEAT

P.T. SILL CUT FROM 2 X ____

SOLID CMU CAP

WD. BLOCKING (REF: STRUCT.)

CPT. O/PLYWD. SHEATHING O/WD. DECK

1 X 3 CVG FIR BASE TRIM

3" X 9" REC. D.F. LEDGER (REF: STRUCT.)

STL. HANGER (REF: STRUCT.)

LINE OF DRYWALL @ UTILITY ROOM

17 SECTION DETAIL
1 1/2" = 1'-0"

CVG FIR WINDOW W/LINER & STANDARD SUBSILL

1/2" X 3" CVG FIR TRIM

PREFIN. MTL. ROOF END WALL TRIM

1/2" X 3" CVG FIR TRIM

MTL. ROOF O/WD. DECK ASSEMBLY

FILENAME.DWG

18 JAMB DETAIL
1 1/2" = 1'-0"

CMU WALL BELOW

CVG SUBSILL (CUSTOM) BY WINDOW MANUF. WRAP AROUND POST

5/4" X 5/4" CVG FIR TRIM

CVG FIR WINDOW W/ LINER BY WINDOW MANUF.

5/4" X FIR TRIM

SUBSILL FLUSH W/TRIM

1 X 3 CEDAR BATTEN

1/2" X CVG FIR TRIM

1/2" X 3" CVG FIR TRIM

19 JAMB DETAIL
1 1/2" = 1'-0"

STUD

EDGE OF CMU WALL BELOW

CMU WALL

REF: _ FOR TYP. NOTES & DIMS.

Michaels/Sisson Residence

Mercer Island, Washington

Situated on a steeply sloping, wooded site alongside a small stream, this residence includes two main stories above a two-story concrete block base containing service spaces. An industrial palette of materials—steel, concrete block, and metal siding—were chosen not only for aesthetic appeal, but also for ease of maintenance.

The concrete block base acts structurally as a stiffened box to retain a fifteen-foot (five-meter) cut into the steep site. The box raises the main living spaces up off the forest floor to increase access to light and air. An expressed steel moment-frame with large wood windows maximizes views into all levels of the forest. One bay of the four-square moment-frame contains a large vertical lift door that opens the house to the site, blurring the boundary between inside and out. At that point, a deck connects the house to the steep hill, providing a level outdoor platform among the trees.

An entry stair tower alongside the garage is cantilevered to prevent damage to the roots of existing Douglas fir trees on the site. This stair leads visitors past the first floor which contains two children's bedrooms, a bathroom, a small play area, laundry, and mechanical storage. As one continues up the stairs, the landing widens to provide space for a small computer area outside of the path of circulation. The upper two stories cantilever off the lower-level garage and bedrooms in an effort to minimize the building footprint on the site. Large sliding panels in the main spaces open up rooms to each other and the outside, creating the feel of an area larger than actually is contained, and forming a living space within the trees.

Above: The upper two stories cantilever off the lower level garage and bedrooms in an effort to minimize the building footprint on the site. On the main level, the kitchen, living, and dining areas open onto a deck with an expansive view of the wooded ravine.

Opposite Page: The entry stair leads visitors past the first floor, which contains mechanical storage, a bathroom, laundry, two purposefully cubby-like children's bedrooms to be completed with built-in furniture and a small play area.

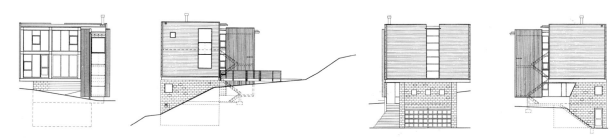

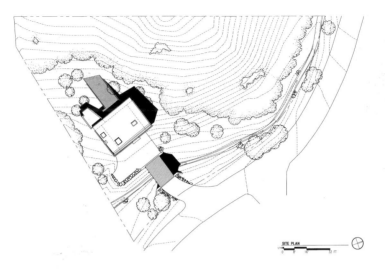

1. Children's Room   7. Dining
2. Bath   8. Kitchen
3. Playroom   9. Music Room
4. Laundry   10. Master Bedroom
5. Entry   11. Study
6. Living

SITE PLAN

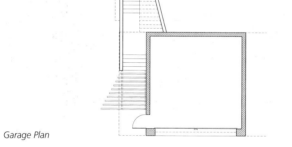

Garage Plan

Second Floor Plan

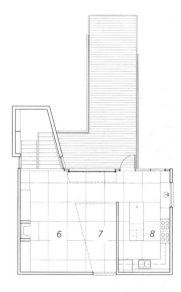

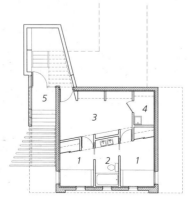

First Floor Plan

Third Floor Plan

Right: *Pressed-fiber flooring panels, prefabricated cabinets, conduit railing cables, exposed slabs and other low-maintenance materials are used for many interior finishes. The upper floor contains space for a music studio and connects to the master bedroom via a bridge overlooking the living space below.*

Opposite Page: *To maintain privacy, the majority of windows face the front and back of the property rather than the neighbors. Large sliding panels in the main spaces open up rooms to each other and the large vertical lift door opens the house to the back deck.*

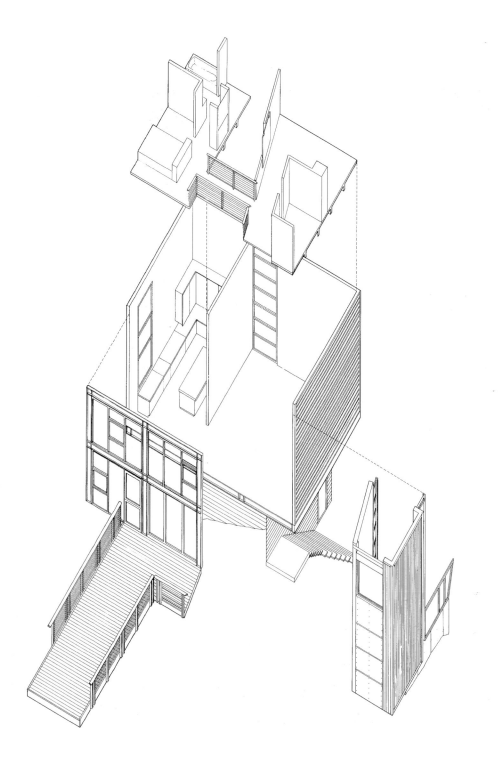

Island Cabin

Decatur Island, Washington

This structure was designed as a second residence for a family of four. The 1,550-square-foot (144-square-meter) cabin is sited in a 100-foot (31-meter) diameter circle on Decatur Island, which was selected for its privacy, views, and need to preserve the existing trees. The island is accessed by a small passenger ferry from the mainland coast city of Anacortes and therefore, construction materials were transported to the rocky shore below the site by barge and hand-carried to the building location.

The design concept breaks the structures into three parts: the main house and the studio/guest house, separated by an exterior glass-covered porch. The porch becomes the main vertical link through the steep site, connecting the pedestrian access road, house, cliff, and beach. This exterior link space serves as the mud room and entry; a sliding, translucent glass barn door screens it from the road on the north. In contrast to the solid north elevation of the cabin, the main living space opens south to the view through two very large glass sliding doors each nine feet (three meters) high by six feet (two meters) wide, converting the space to an outdoor room. No visible beams or headers interrupt this operable window wall, which supports an adjacent cantilevered door with light steel rods.

Above: When the large glass doors are open, the main living space is enclosed as much by the nearby madrona trees as by the deck railing.

Opposite Page: Roof supports mirror the surrounding madrona tree branches while allowing a roof cantilever sufficient to protect the glazing and the deck on this facade.

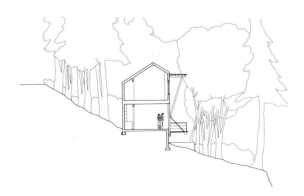

Section Facing East

Site Plan

1. Main House

2. Guest House/Studio

3. Glass Covered Porch

4. Deck

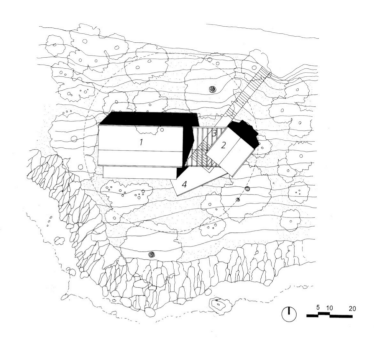

Upper Floor Plan

1. Main Bedroom

2. Children's Bedroom

3. Guest Area

4. Glass-Covered Porch

Lower Floor Plan

5. Kitchen

6. Dining Room

7. Living Room

8. Studio

9. Covered Porch

10. Deck

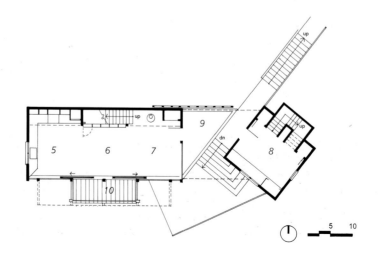

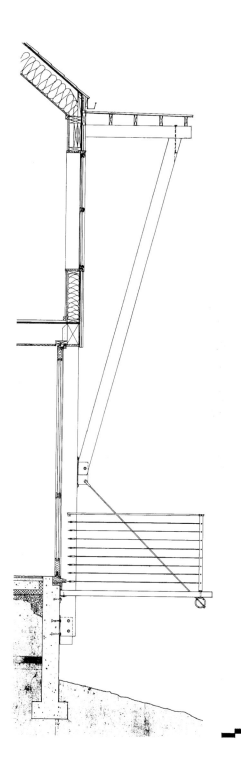

12 24

Above: *Clearly articulated details that both aesthetically and physically reinforce their function are seen most easily in the deck structure.*

Opposite Page: *Board and batten cedar siding that changes in scale between the house and studio both reinforces the separation of functions and ties the building together. The glazed roof above the entry deck provides shelter for exterior uses.*

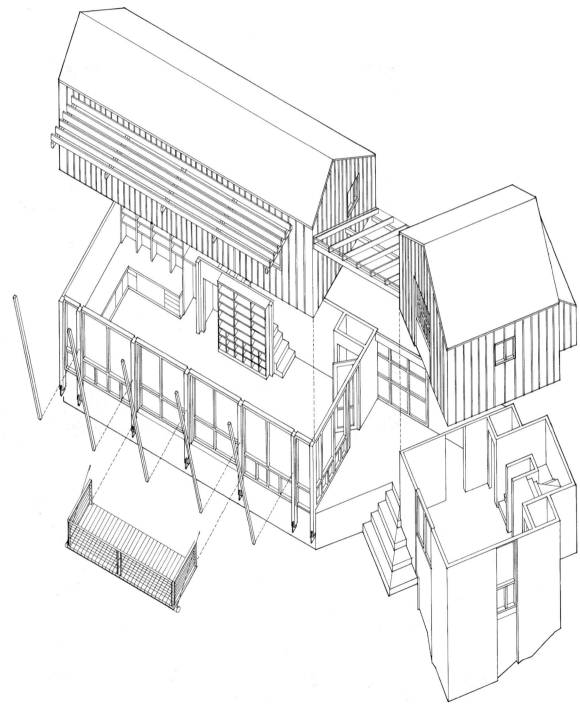

Selected Buildings and Projects

Camarda Residence
Vashon Island, Washington

Team: Craig Curtis, Amy Lelyveld
Site: 5 acres (2 ha)
Building: 2,200 sf (204 sm)
Completed: Fall 1994

The Miller/Hull Partnership
Architectural Staff 1988–1998

David Miller, Partner
Robert Hull, Partner
Norman Strong, Partner
Craig Curtis, Partner
Sarah Sian Roberts, Associate
Stephen Southerland, Associate
Steven Tatge, Associate
Scott Wolf, Associate
Mark Adams
Chris Arthur
Dave Brunner
Allison Capen
Victoria Carter
Lené Copeland
Philip Christofides
Susana Covarrubias
Amy DeDominicis
Laurie Fanger
Allan Farkas
Laura Hafermann
Gabriel Hajiani
Annie Han
Robert Hutchison
Susan Kelly
Lisa Kirkendall
Steve de Koch
Julie Kreigh
Olivier Landa
Amy Lelyveld
Claudine Manio
Rhonda Mauer
Andrew Michal
Daniel Mihalyo
Doug Mikko
Renae Nelson
Christopher Patano
Chad Rollins
Cathi Scott
Teresa Shannon
Ted Shelton
Tracy Smith
Aidan Stretch
Tricia Stuth
Mark Vanderzanden
Richard Whealan
Holden Withington
Peter Wolff

Novotny Cabin
Decatur Island, Washington

Team: Robert Hull, Craig Curtis
Site: 100-foot (30-meter) diameter circle
Building: 840 sf (78 sm)
Completed: Fall 1990

Grand Coulee Residence
Electric City, Washington

Team: David Miller, Amy Lelyveld
Site: 2 acres (0.8 ha)
Building: 1,200 sf (111 sm)
Completed: Fall 1995

Campbell Residence
Yakima Valley, Washington

Team: Craig Curtis, Sian Roberts
Site: 180 acres (73 ha)
Building: 1,350 sf (125 sm)
Completed: Spring 1998

Gorton/Bounds Cabin
Decatur Island, Washington

Team: Robert Hull, Jeff Cook
Site: 100-foot (30-meter) diameter circle
Building: 600 sf (56 sm)
Completed: Fall 1987

Bainbridge House and Studio
Bainbridge Island, Washington

Team: David Miller, Craig Curtis, Victoria Carter
Site: 2.5 acres (1 ha)
Building: House—2,600 sf (252 sm); Studio—1,000 sf (93 sm)
Completed: Spring 1993

Michaels/Sisson Residence
Mercer Island, Washington

Team: Robert Hull, Amy DeDominicis
Site: 2.5 acres (1 ha)
Building: 2,400 sf (223 sm)
Completed: Fall 1998

Marquand Retreat
Naches River Valley, Washington

Team: David Miller, Philip Christofides
Site: 200 acres (81 ha)
Building: 450 sf (42 sm)
Completed: November 1992

Ching Cabin
Maury Island, Washington

Team: David Miller, Rob Hutchison
Site: 10 acres (4 ha)
Building: House—600 sf (56 sm); Shed—300 sf (28 sm)
Completed: Fall 1998

Island Cabin
Decatur Island, Washington

Team: Robert Hull, Victoria Carter
Site: 100-foot (31-meter) diameter circle
Building: Main house—1,550 sf (144 sm); Guest house—400 sf (37 sm)
Completed: Fall 1994

Firm Profile

The Miller/Hull Partnership has built a reputation based on simple, elegant, and authentic designs. The Seattle firm, established in 1977, has pursued a rigorous logic in its design approach, which is based on the belief that architectural programs are best solved directly and efficiently. This rigor has resulted in a body of work that expresses powerful concepts in lyrical form.

Founding partners David Miller and Robert Hull, both raised in Washington State, have explored the development of two dominant themes in America's western regional architecture: the need to establish a defined place within the landscape, and the art of rational building. Their attitude toward building in the landscape takes advantage of a mutual inflection in which architecture and landscape seem to need each other for completion. In their residential architecture they attempt to capture the spirit and vitality of the American West by focusing on the tensions between nature and materiality, detail, and structure.

Miller/Hull has developed a community-based architecture for a variety of clients ranging from regional governmental agencies, colleges, and universities to private corporations and residential owners. They have been the recipient of more than seventy national and regional design awards during their first twenty years of practice. Their design work has been frequently published in international journals, has been featured in exhibitions—including two solo shows—and has been the subject of lectures given by the firm's Partners in the United States, Canada, Japan, and Italy. The office currently has a staff of twenty-four and added two partners in addition to Miller and Hull: Norman Strong (1986) and Craig Curtis (1994).

The firm will always work within the modern tradition: a tradition they see as evolving, rather than static. The Miller/Hull Partnership strives to make a significant contribution to a richer modernism.

Photographic Credits

Ernest Braun
Mercy Residence p. 9

Steven Cridland
Marquand Retreat pp. 36, 40, 44

Ernie Duncan
Campbell Residence pp. 7, 82, 83 top, 84–86

Chris Eden: Eden Arts
Gorton/Bounds Cabin pp. 26, 28–32, 34, 35
Camarda Residence pp. 72, 75 top, 76, 78, 79
Island Cabin cover, pp. 2, 6, 98, 102–105

Art Grice
Bainbridge House and Studio p. 63 bottom
Ching Cabin pp. 64, 65, 66 bottom, 67 top, 68–70
Michaels/Sisson Residence pp. 94 top, 95–97

Fred Housel
Model Photographs pp. 8–11, 12 bottom two rows, 13
Poschman Residence p. 14 bottom
Marquand Retreat p. 38
Grand Coulee Residence pp. 46–49
Bainbridge House and Studio pp. 54, 56, 62
Ching Cabin p. 67 bottom
Campbell Residence pp. 80, 81, 83 bottom, 88–91
Michaels/Sisson Residence cover, pp. 92, 93, 94 bottom

Miller/Hull
Marquand Retreat pp. 7 bottom right, 37, 39, 42, 43
Roundy Residence p. 11 top
Grande Ronde Ranch p. 12 top row
Poschman Residence pp. 14 top and center, 15
Novotny Cabin pp. 17, 18
Gorton/Bounds Cabin p. 27
Grand Coulee Residence pp. 50, 51
Camarda Residence p. 74 bottom
Bainbridge House and Studio pp. 55, 63 top
Island Cabin pp. 99, 100

Undine Prohl
Camarda Residence pp. 7 bottom left, 73, 74 top, 75 bottom
Ching Cabin p. 66 top

Michael Skott
Island Cabin p. 101

Michael Shopenn
Novotny Cabin pp. 16, 19–25
Bainbridge House and Studio pp. 52, 53, 58, 60, 61